Managing Editor
Ina Massler Levin, M.A.

Editor
Heather Douglas

Contributing Editor
Sarah Smith

Creative Director
Karen J. Goldfluss, M.S. Ed.

Cover Design
Tony Carrillo / Marilyn Goldberg

Teacher Created Resources, Inc.
12621 Western Avenue
Garden Grove, CA 92841
www.teachercreated.com

ISBN: 978-1-4206-5976-4

©2007 Teacher Created Resources, Inc.
Reprinted, 2021 (PO603209)

Made in U.S.A.

This book belongs to

_____

Ready·Set·Learn

Get Ready to Learn!

Get ready, get set, and go! Boost your child's learning with this exciting series of books. Geared to help children practice and master many needed skills, the *Ready·Set·Learn* books are bursting with 64 pages of learning fun. Use these books for . . .

✸ enrichment　　✸ skills reinforcement　　✸ extra practice

With their smaller size, the *Ready·Set·Learn* books fit easily in children's hands, backpacks, and book bags. All your child needs to get started are pencils, crayons, and colored pencils.

A full sheet of colorful stickers is included. Use these stickers for . . .

✸ decorating pages

✸ rewarding outstanding effort

✸ keeping track of completed pages

Celebrate your child's progress by using these stickers on the reward chart located on the inside cover. The blue-ribbon sticker fits perfectly on the certificate on page 64.

With *Ready·Set·Learn* and a little encouragement, your child will be on the fast track to learning fun!

Catch the Dog

Directions: Help Officer Fritz catch Runaway Dog! Find your way through the maze with a pencil. Color the pictures with a crayon.

4

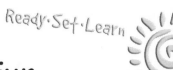

Boxes of Fun

Directions: Draw a line from each box to its matching lid.

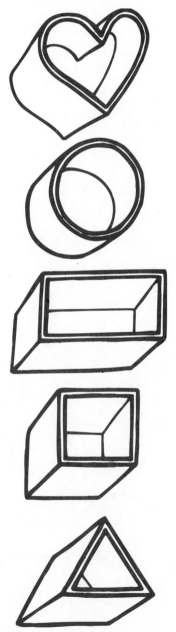

Vroom!

Directions: Trace the lines to finish the pictures. Color the cars.

6

What's Missing?

Directions: Fill in the missing parts on each snowman to make them all the same.

Number Patterns

Directions: Look at each line of number patterns. Write the missing number on each line to complete the pattern.

1 2 3 1 2 1 2 __

6 9 6 9 __ 9

5 7 7 5 7 __

3 4 __ 3 4 5

9 __ 9 8 9 8

Color Words

Directions: Trace the color words on each crayon. Color the crayons to match the color words.

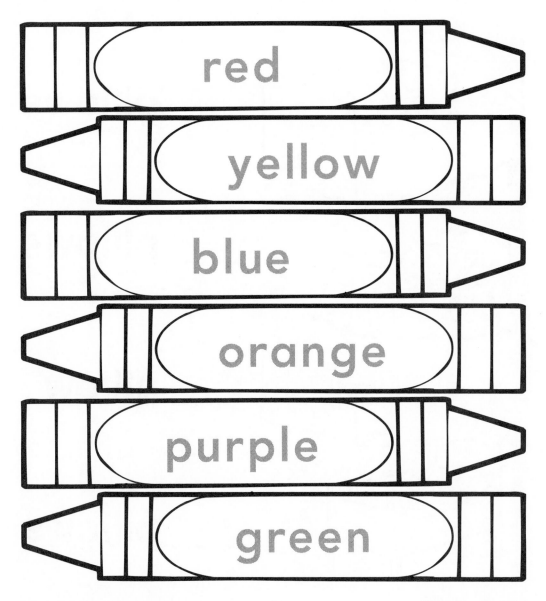

red

yellow

blue

orange

purple

green

How Long?

Directions: Count the pillows on each bed. Write the number on the line next to each bed. Circle the bed with the most pillows. That is the longest bed.

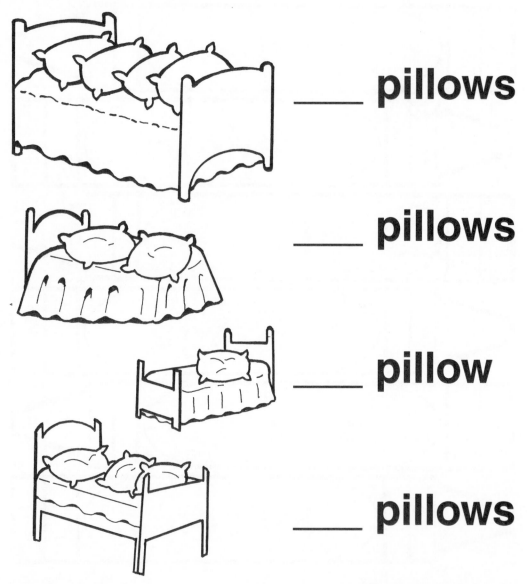

____ **pillows**

____ **pillows**

____ **pillow**

____ **pillows**

10

Maze

Directions: Help the teacher find her desk. Draw a line from the teacher to her desk.

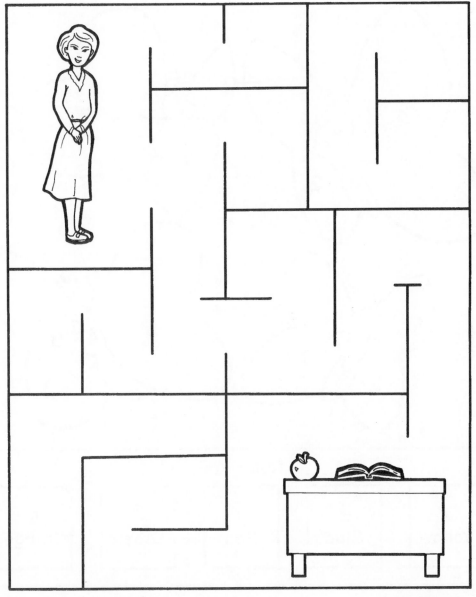

Color Codes

Directions: Color the Color Key. Color the picture using the Color Key.

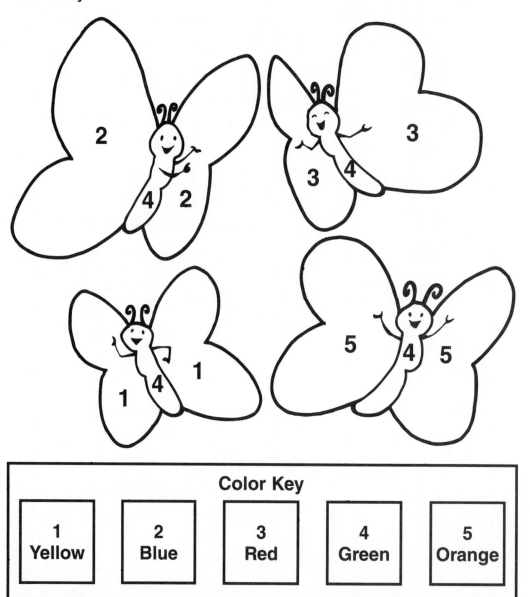

Color Key

1 Yellow	2 Blue	3 Red	4 Green	5 Orange

12 ©Teacher Created Resources, Inc.

Apples

Directions: Color the apples red.

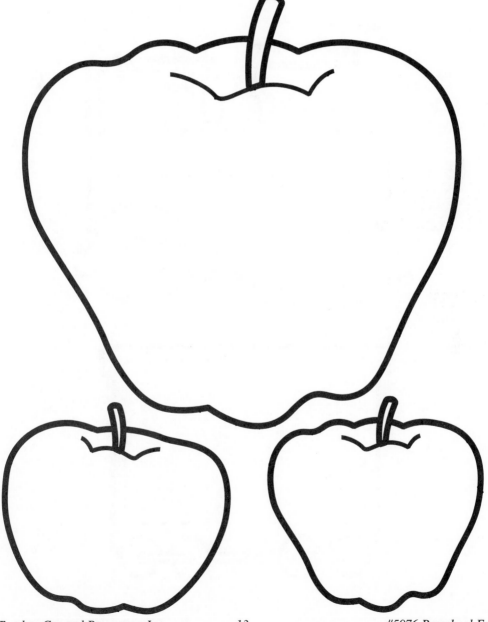

Making Rectangles

Directions: Trace on the dotted lines to form the rectangle shapes within the picture.

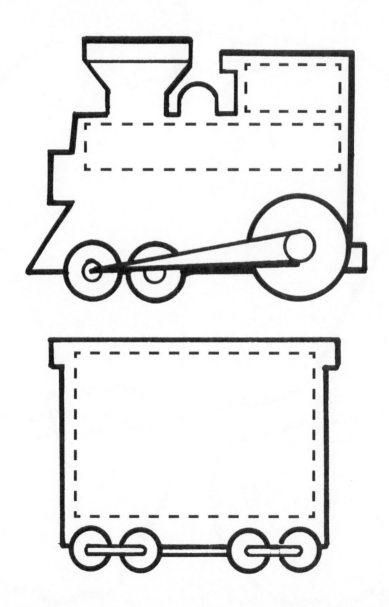

I Can Count

1. Trace your hand.
2. Color it.
3. Count your fingers.
4. Draw a line from each fingers to a number.

3

2

4

1

5

Stained Glass Picture

Directions: Color the Color Key. Color each section of stained glass picture using the Color Key. What do you see?

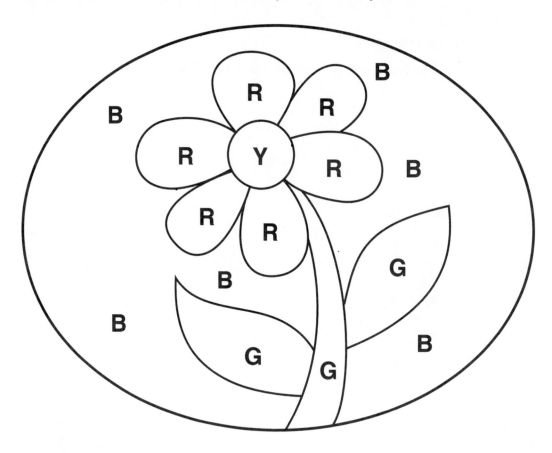

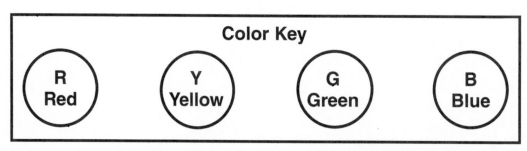

Different Dinosaurs

Directions: Count each type of dinosaur. Graph the total for each.

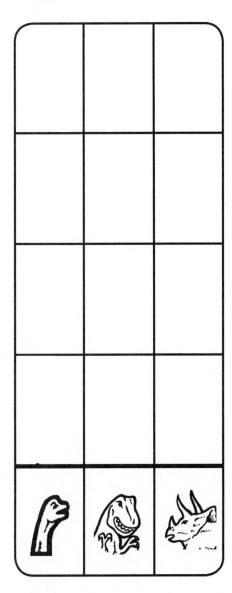

Circles

Directions: Trace the gray circles. Practice making your own circles by adding more balloons and string.

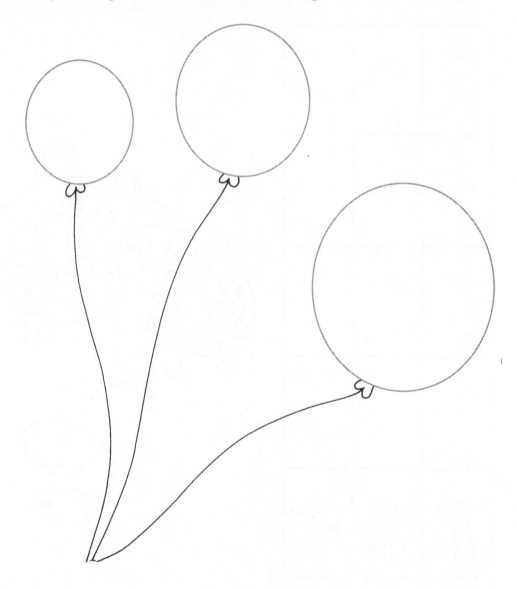

Flower Power

Directions: Trace the line and circle to finish the picture. Color the flower.

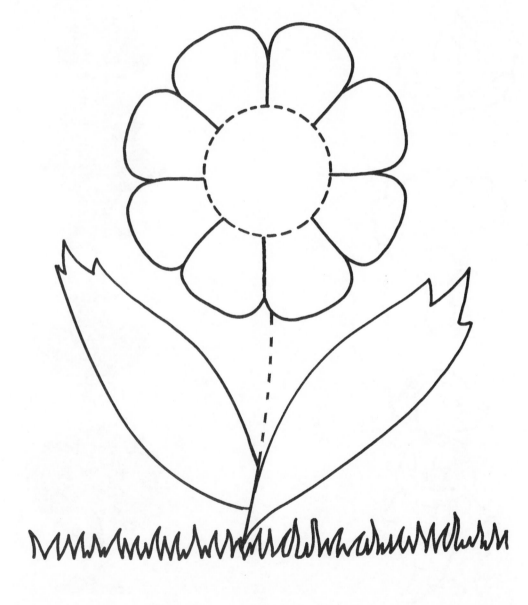

Shadows

Directions: Draw a line from each object to its shadow. Color the pictures with crayons.

20

Beach Ball Alphabet

Directions: Fill in the missing letters.

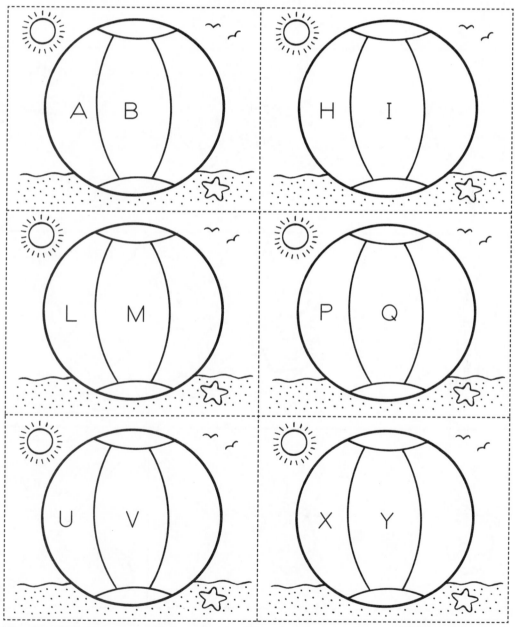

Plenty of Patterns

Directions: Look at each pattern. Circle which picture comes next in the pattern. Color the sequence.

Ice Cream

Directions: Color the ice cream cone.

Draw a Fish

Directions: Follow the steps to draw a fish in the blank box. Color your fish.

Diamond

Directions: Trace on the dotted line to form the diamond shape within the picture.

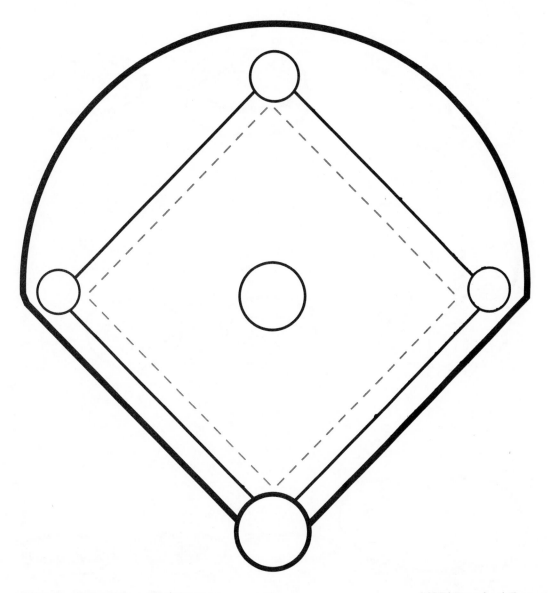

Who's Got More?

Directions: Look at each pet's bowl. Circle the bowl that has the most food.

 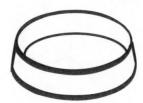 

  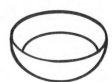

Jack and the Beanstalk

Directions: Draw green leaves on the *tallest* beanstalk.

Color by Number

Directions: Color all the 4's brown. Color all the 5's green.

Counting Buttons

Directions: Someone forgot to put on the snowmen's buttons. Finish the snowmen by drawing on the correct numbers and colors of buttons.

2 blue buttons   **4 black buttons**

Teddy Bear

Directions: Color the teddy bear brown.

Day and Night

Directions: In the first box, draw a picture of something you do at night. In the second box, draw a picture of something you do during the day.

Night

Day

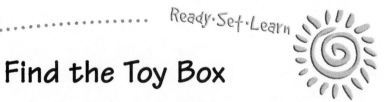

Find the Toy Box

Directions: Help the teddy bear find the toy box. Find your way through the maze with a pencil. Color the pictures.

Pumpkin

Directions: Color the pumpkin orange.

Hungry Gators

Directions: Circle the set that has more for each alligator.

34

Complete the Pictures

Directions: Look at each picture carefully. Some things are missing. Complete each picture. Color the dog and the house.

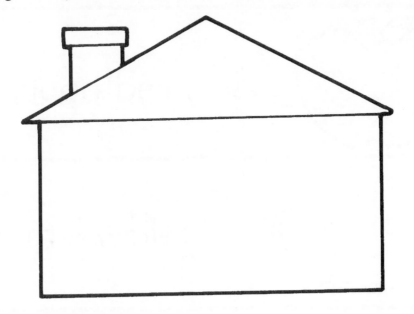

Colors

Directions: Color each object.

red apple

yellow lemon

orange pumpkin

blue blueberries

In the Rain, I Wear . . .

Directions: Start at 1 and connect the dots to complete the picture. What is it? Color your picture.

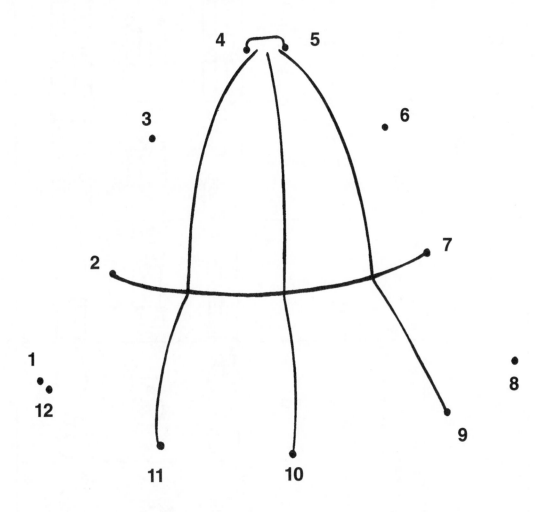

Presents

Directions: Trace the numbers. Color the correct number of presents in each row.

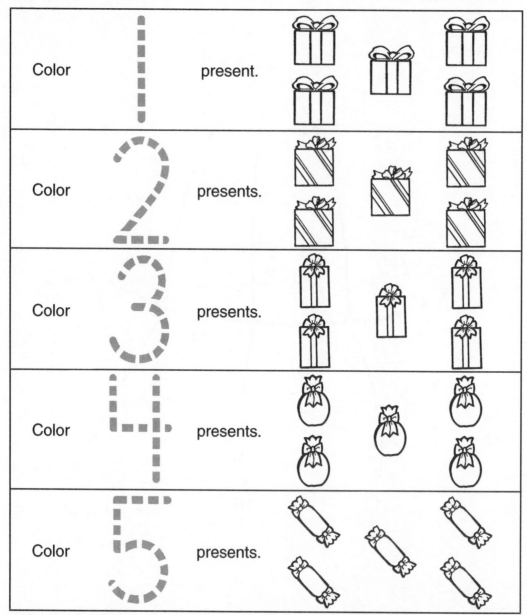

Gilberto's Balloons

Directons: Draw 5 balloons for Gilberto. Color 2 red. Color 3 blue.

What Comes Next?

Directions: Look at each pattern. Color the picture that comes next.

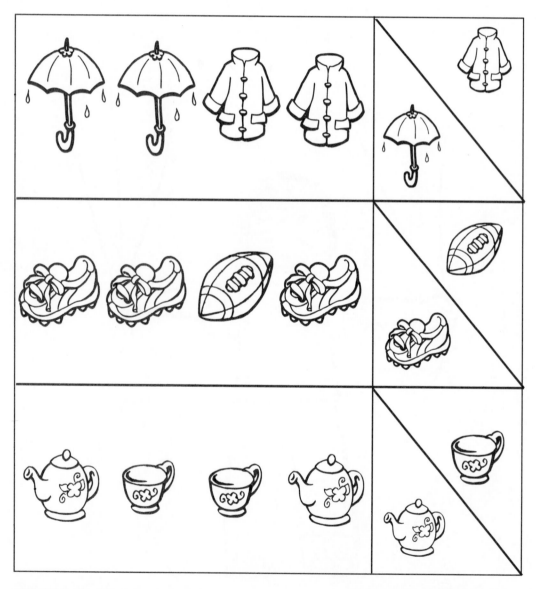

Autumn Leaf

Directions: Color the oak leaf yellow.

Beach Finds

Directions: Look at the list of items to find at the bottom of the page. Count the items and write the number on the line next to the picture. Color the picture.

Matching Mittens

Directions: Draw a line to match each pair of mittens. Color the mittens with crayons. Use the same colors for each pair.

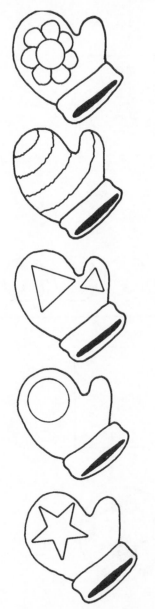

Ball Tally

Directions: Count each type of sports ball. Write the number in the box.

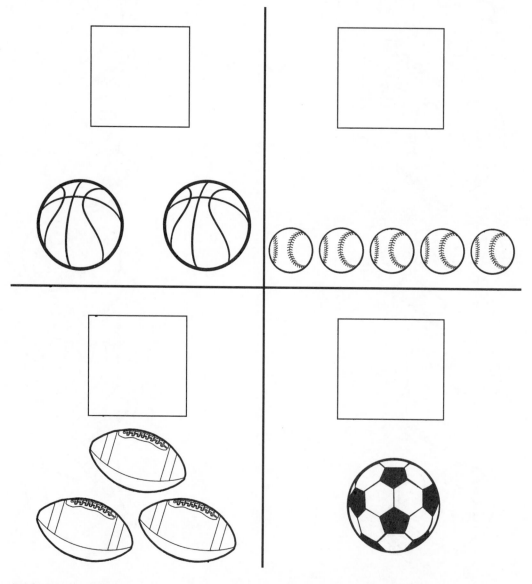

Draw a Cat

Directions: Follow the steps to draw a big cat. Color your cat.

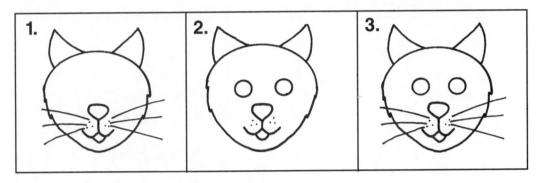

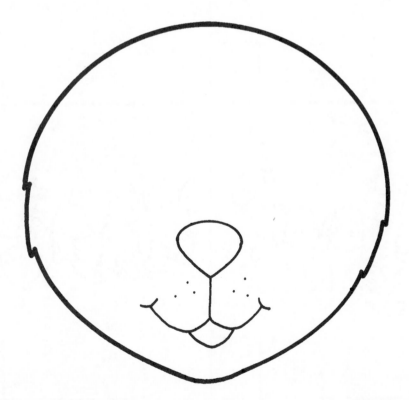

Animal Count

Directions: Look at the animals in each box. Write the number of animals in each space.

46

Hearts

Directions: Color the hearts red.

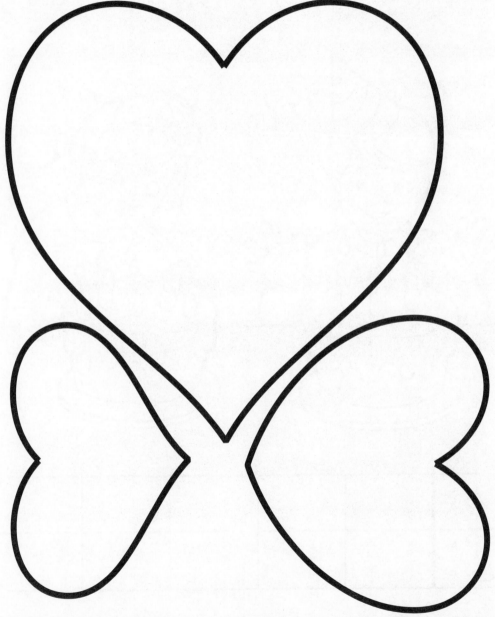

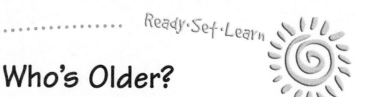

Who's Older?

Directions: Count the candles on each birthday cake. Graph the total for each. Color the birthday cake for the older child.

Find the Ants

Directions: Circle the ants on the page. How many ants did you find?

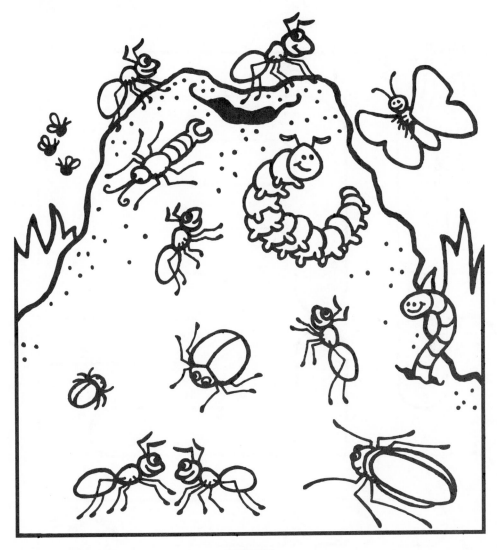

I found ☐ ants.

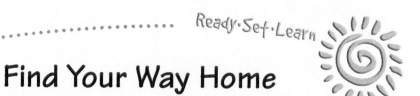

Find Your Way Home

Directions: Help Molly find her way home. Find your way through the maze with a pencil. Color the pictures.

Bees

Directions: Color the bees yellow.

Shapely Monsters

Directions: Count the number of shapes found in each monster. Write each answer on the line next to the shape.

Count the Library Books

Directions: Count the library books in each row. Write the number in the box.

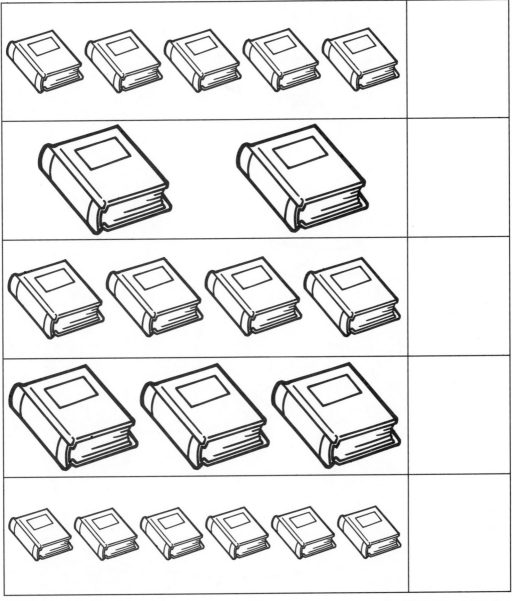

Surprise

Directions: Connect the dots from 1–20 to finish the picture. Color the picture.

54

How Many?

Directions: Use the pictures to answer the questions below.

How many ?_____   How many  ?_____

How many ?_____   How many  ?_____

How many pets in all ?_____   How many balls in all ?_____

Pumpkin Patch Maze

Directions: Help the farmer find his way back to the barn.

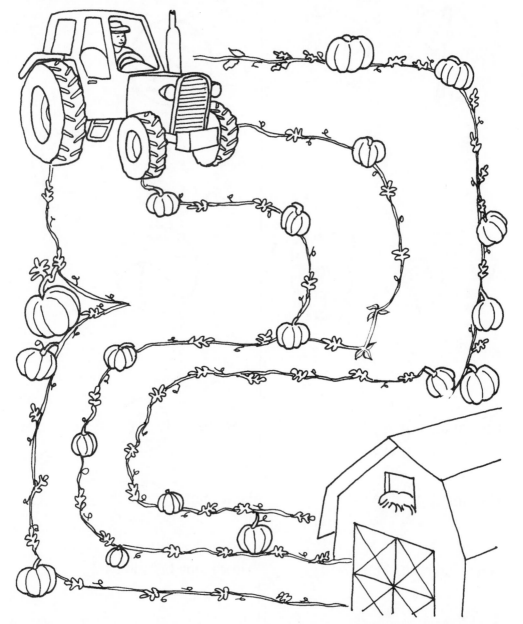

Shamrock

Directions: Color the shamrock green.

Ride Me

1. Connect the dots from 1 to 10.

2. Color me yellow.

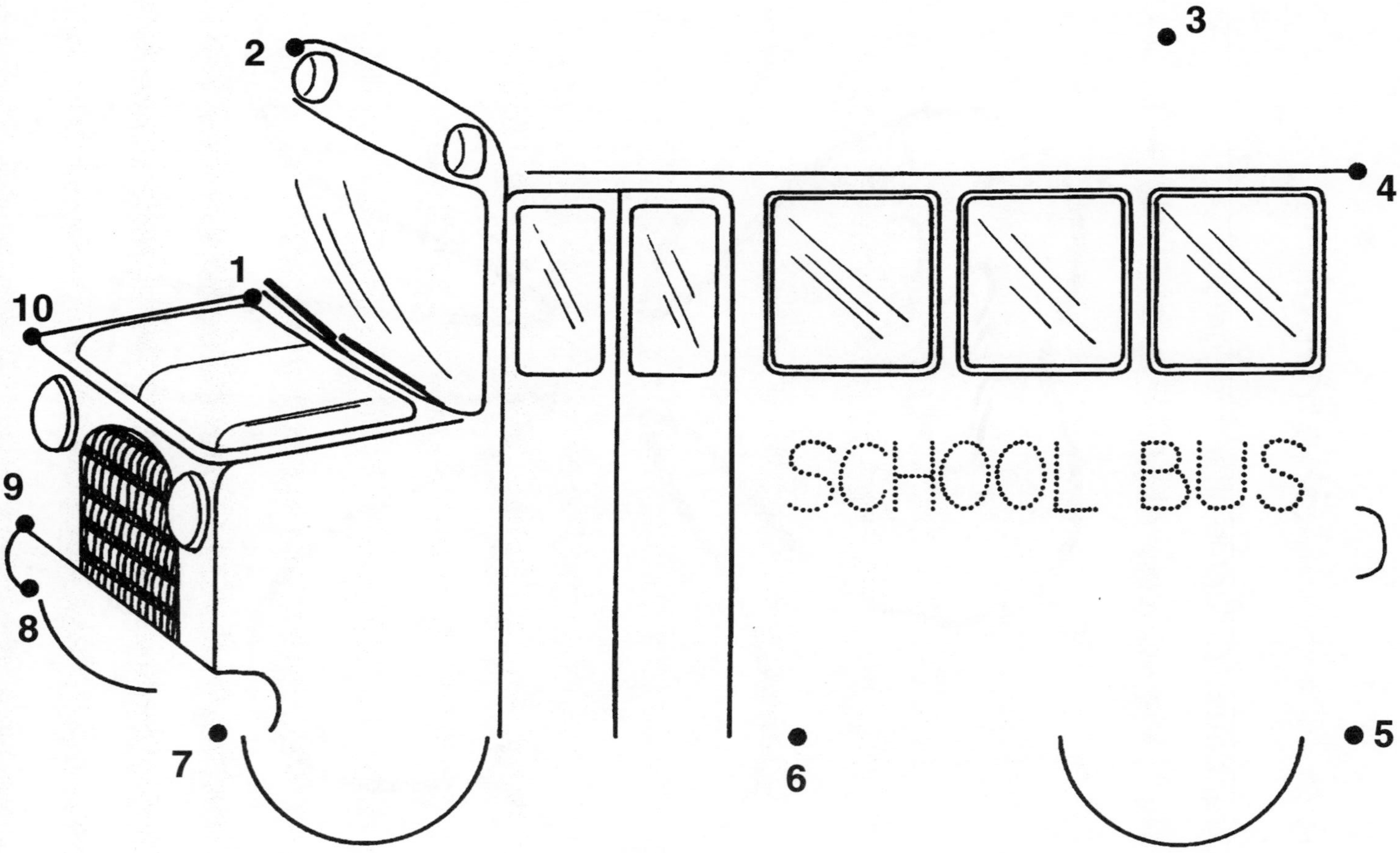

SCHOOL BUS

58

Unicorns

Directions: Unicorns have only one horn. Color the true
unicorns.

Slow and Easy Wins

Directions: Connect the dots from 1–12 to find out who won the race. Color the picture.

60

Mouse

Directions: Give the friendly mouse a long thin tail.

Family Portrait

Directions: Draw a picture inside the frame of all the people who live in your house.

This Award
Is Presented To

_____

for

★ Doing Your Best

★ Trying Hard

★ Not Giving Up

★ Making a
Great Effort